MW00681557

# Goddess Rituals

# Goddess Rituals

## INVOKE THE POWERS OF THE GODDESSES TO IMPROVE YOUR LIFE

**RONI JAY**

Illustrations by
Carole Hènaff

STERLING ETHOS
New York

STERLING ETHOS
New York

An Imprint of Sterling Publishing Co., Inc.
1166 Avenue of the Americas
New York, NY 10036

ISBN 978-1-4549-3475-2

Distributed in Canada by
Sterling Publishing Co., Inc., c/o
Canadian Manda Group, 664 Annette Street,
Toronto, Ontario M6S 2C8, Canada

For information about custom editions,
special sales, and premium and corporate
purchases, please contact Sterling
Special Sales at 800-805-5489 or
specialsales@sterlingpublishing.com.

Manufactured in China

10 9 8 7 6 5 4 3 2 1

sterlingpublishing.com

Conceived, edited, and designed by
Quarto Publishing plc, an imprint of
The Quarto Group
6 Blundell Street
London N7 9BH

QUAR.326291

Editor: Claire Waite Brown
Senior Designer: Martina Calvio
Designer: Karin Skånberg
Art Director: Jess Hibbert
Publisher: Samantha Warrington

# CONTENTS

**INTRODUCTION 6**

**GODDESSES AND RITUALS 10**

**ASTARTE 12**
*Safety through the night 14*
*Relaxation 15*

**ATHENA 16**
*Wisdom 18*
*Artistic success 19*

**BASTET 20**
*Gentleness 23*
*Protection from nightmares 24*

**CHALCHIUHTLICUE 26**
*Marriage 28*
*Protecting newborn babies 29*

**DIANA 30**
*Chastity 32*
*Childbirth 33*

**EPONA 34**
*Healing 36*
*Caring for animals 37*

**EZILI 38**
*Sexual love 41*
*Prosperity 43*

**FRIGGA 44**
*Good fortune 46*
*Protection from danger 47*

**GAIA 48**
*Empathy with nature 50*
*Oaths 51*

**HATHOR 52**
*Guarding children's future 54*
*Foreign travel 55*

**HEL 56**
*Easing sickness 59*
*Bereavement 60*

**HERA 62**
*Protection from infidelity 64*
*Strength in times of conflict 65*

**ISHTAR 66**
*Sexual passion 68*
*Faithfulness 69*

**ISIS 70**
*Loyalty 73*
*Pregnancy 74*
*Motherhood 75*

**KUAN YIN 76**
*Compassion 78*
*Purity 79*

**LAKSHMI 80**
*Happiness 82*
*Beginning a project 83*

**MAAT 84**
*Truth 86*
*Justice 87*

**NUT 88**
*Infertility 91*
*Gaining time 92*

**PAPA 94**
*Divorce 96*
*Conflict with children 99*

**PARVATI 100**
*Support in partnership 102*
*Persistence 103*

**PROSERPINA 104**
*Patience 106*
*Sunny weather 107*

**SEDNA 108**
*Forgiveness 110*
*Searching 111*

**TARA 112**
*Insight into a lover's heart 114*
*Safety in travel 115*

**VENUS 116**
*Separation in love 119*
*Welcoming the spring 121*

**XOCHIQUETZAL 122**
*Singing and dancing 124*
*Success in craftsmanship 125*

*Index 126*

# INTRODUCTION

Since the dawn of time, humans have worshipped a vast pantheon of goddesses, invoking their help in times of need and offering thanks in times of plenty. Each civilization developed its own cast of goddesses, often with remarkable similarities, and always including mother and fertility goddesses as well as goddesses of love, compassion, and wisdom. Whether you believe that there are many different goddesses, or whether you believe that these goddesses are simply aspects of one great deity, it is easier to empathize with an individual goddess—or just one of the great goddess's aspects—when you need help or guidance. The question is: which is the right goddess for you at this moment in time?

This book introduces you to goddesses from all over the world, so that you can choose the one you feel most comfortable approaching, and who has particular significance to your problem or request. Each goddess has her own area of patronage—love, leadership, creativity, and so on—so you can call on different goddesses in different situations.

## GODDESSES AND THEIR RITUALS

The goddesses are selected from around the world, and range from Diana, the virgin goddess of Roman mythology who protects women in childbirth, to the Mesopotamian Ishtar, goddess of war and sexual love, and the patroness of harlots. You will find the Scandinavian goddess of the underworld, Hel, who is responsible for those who die of sickness or old age, and the beautiful Chinese goddess of compassion and mercy, Kuan Yin, who looks after newlyweds.

From among these goddesses, you are bound to find one with whom you feel a special empathy, or whose sphere of influence is particularly significant to your life. Read through each goddess's history until you have identified the goddess—or goddesses—whom you wish to call on for help and strength.

The rituals associated with the various goddesses encompass many different situations: for emotional needs such as wisdom and patience; for well-being, such as good fortune and relaxation; for love and marriage, covering everything from engendering sexual passion to gaining strength during a divorce; concerning children, from infertility to childbirth; and for activities, from traveling to dancing, and gaining time to settling disputes.

Each of the rituals calls on a goddess who has a particular interest in the subject of the ritual. So, for example, you would call on Hathor, the Egyptian goddess associated with foreign lands, to support you when traveling abroad; or on the earth goddess Gaia to give you greater empathy with nature.

## OBJECTS OF FOCUS

The rituals usually incorporate objects on which to focus. These are generally everyday things that are not hard to find (although a little effort can be a good thing). For instance, you might need an apple or a length of pink ribbon. If you cannot find the objects specified in the ritual, don't worry: simply substitute them with the closest you can find. Ideally, the objects should be made of natural substances, so use cotton or silk ribbon rather than nylon, for example; if a bowl of water is needed, then use a simple bowl of metal or clay, rather than a plastic one.

## CREATING THE MOOD

For all the rituals in this book you should be in a calm and focused state of mind, so you will need to follow a few simple guidelines.

✳ Do not perform any of these rituals when you are in a hurry. Make sure you set aside plenty of time—most of them will not take more than ten or twenty minutes.

✳ You should be alone when you are performing the ritual, or with the other person or persons performing the ritual with you. There should not be anyone present who is not taking part in the ritual.

✳ Make sure that you will not be disturbed. Prevent interruptions by turning off cell phone and computer notifications.

✳ Try to perform the ritual in a quiet place. Avoid, or at least minimize, background noise, apart from any sounds or music required by the ritual itself. Switch off the radio or television, and close the windows if it is noisy outside.

## DEVELOPING NEW RITUALS

Once you become adept at using rituals regularly in times of need, there is no reason why you should not develop others of your own to help with situations that are not included in this book. Follow the guidelines above, making sure that the ritual you devise directs your focus toward your chosen goddess and the situation for which you are requesting her strength.

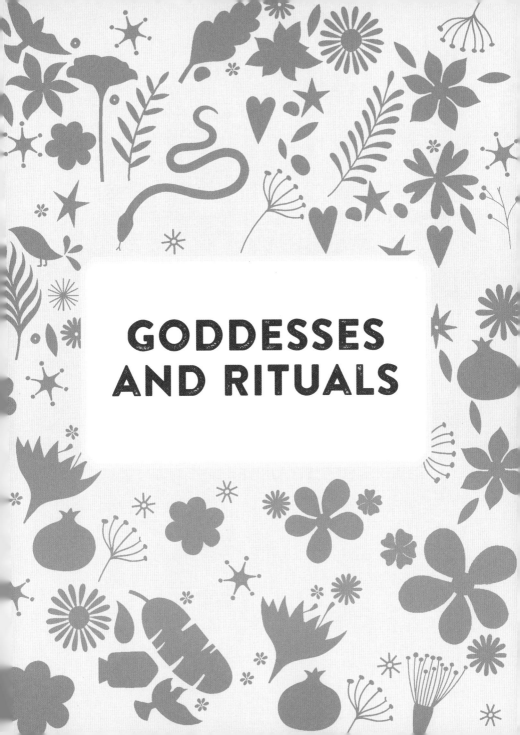

# GODDESSES
# AND RITUALS

# ASTARTE

*Phoenician goddess of the moon, war, and love*

Astarte is the Phoenician mother goddess, the evening star, and is usually depicted naked. Her animal is the sphinx, and she is frequently shown seated on a throne flanked by a pair of sphinxes. She often wears a crown made of cow's horns surrounding a sun disk, just like that of the Egyptian mother goddess, Hathor.

Astarte is full of passion, seduction, and sexual abandon. She is lustful, and her cult followers often indulged in orgiastic rites. Her important temples were in Tyre, Carthage, and Cyprus, and she is mentioned in the Bible as the Sidonian goddess, since the kings of Sidon were her priests.

Astarte appears in different guises as the wife of both Baal and El. As the wife of the rain god Baal, she is the ferocious Anat; she also takes the form of Athirat, lady of the sea, as wife to the great father god El. As Anat, Astarte saved Baal when he was killed by the god of death, Mot. She descended to the underworld and viciously attacked and killed Mot, using a sickle and shovel to cut him, fire to scorch him, and a mill to grind him up. Finally, she scattered his flesh across the fields as food for the birds. By this means she reversed her husband's fate.

# SAFETY THROUGH THE NIGHT

*Astarte's symbol is the moon, and she therefore rules over the night, so she is an appropriate goddess to invoke to keep you safe as you sleep. You can also adapt this ritual to call upon Astarte to watch over your partner, your children, or even your cat or dog while they sleep.*

## YOU WILL NEED

- A small talisman that represents the moon
- A small box or drawstring pouch

**PREPARATION**

Perform this ritual at night when there is a full moon. Stand in front of an open window through which the moon is shining, or stand outside in the moonlight.

-

The talisman you choose to represent the moon could be a white pearl, a silver bead, or a glass marble.

1 Looking at the full moon, place one hand on top of the other, palm upward, and cup the talisman in your upturned hands.

2 Focus your mind and call on Astarte: "Astarte, goddess of the moon, fill this sphere with your light and protection."

3 Place the talisman in the box or pouch, and put it under your pillow or mattress, or under that of the person you want Astarte to protect.

## RITUAL

# RELAXATION

*Astarte is the spirit of the evening star, so she is an appropriate goddess to invoke at the end of the day if you are feeling stressed and anxious.*

### YOU WILL NEED

· Candles
· Scented oils

**BATHING RITUAL**
This ritual involves running yourself a warm bath containing sensual, scented oils, and bathing by candlelight.

1 Light as many candles as you would like and pour yourself a bath scented with oils of your choice.

2 Before you get into the bathtub, stand beside it and say: "Astarte, help me to end this day more content than I began it."

3 Now step into the bath. Wash yourself all over, then lie back and enjoy the feel of the warm water around you.

4 Close your eyes and breathe deeply. Concentrate on your breath going in and out, and your chest rising and falling. Let any tension slip away.

5 When you feel really relaxed, keep your eyes closed and think about the day you have had, going through it mentally from when you awoke that morning. Reflect on what you have experienced during the course of the day, and try to itemize the things you have achieved, large or small, personal, educational, or spiritual. Do not open your eyes until you have thought of at least three things, so that you can end your day with a sense of achievement.

6 After your bath, go straight to bed.

# ATHENA

*Greek goddess of war, wisdom, and the arts*

Athena was not born naturally, but sprang from the head of her father—the supreme god Zeus—fully armed and shouting a war cry. Athena is a virgin, but she enjoys the company of men and often takes their side. Unlike Ares, her counterpart god of war, she sees war as a necessary evil, but does not enjoy its savagery. She is a great strategist and a clever tactician, and favors wisdom above brute strength.

When the gods first divided up the earth between them, Athena and Poseidon (god of the sea) vied for possession of the Attica region of Greece. Poseidon made a spring burst from the rock of the Acropolis, but Athena manifested an olive tree growing on the sacred rock. Zeus judged her the winner, and she gave her name and protection to the city of Athens that grew up around the Acropolis.

Athena's symbol is the owl, and also the skin of the sacrificial goat. She is usually portrayed wearing a coat of mail and a helmet and shield. She is associated with olive trees, and also with many skills—especially spinning and weaving—since she taught men to tame their savage natures and use their intelligence to learn skill at crafts and to appreciate the arts.

## RITUAL

# WISDOM

*Athena was the wisest goddess of all, and we can all benefit from bringing some of her wisdom and insight into our lives. The ancient Greeks traditionally honored Athena on her festival day by dressing in new clothes, as though clothing themselves in her wisdom. The first thing you can do, then, is buy or borrow something new to wear that is fit for a goddess.*

**POLITE PURPLE**

Purple is the traditional color of wisdom, so choose a new item of clothing that features purple, whether all over or with a purple edging or pattern. You could even choose purple jewelry or underwear. It does not have to be prudish, but remember that Athena is a virgin goddess, so do not offend her by wearing anything overtly sexual.

### YOU WILL NEED

- New clothes or jewelry featuring the color purple
- A bowl of olives

1 As you put on your new clothes or jewelry in the morning, imagine that you are clothing yourself in Athena's wisdom.

2 Olives are sacred to Athena, so, at the end of the day, sit down with a bowlful and ask for her help, saying: "As I eat your olives, let me be filled with your wisdom and insight, and keep it with me throughout the year."

3 Eat the olives one at a time, and as you do so, reflect on the areas of your life that will benefit most from Athena's wisdom.

## RITUAL

# ARTISTIC SUCCESS

*If your work is decorative rather than functional, Athena is the goddess to invoke. She governs success in all areas of artistic pursuit, whether your talents lie in writing, sculpting, or embroidery.*

## YOU WILL NEED

• The tools you use in pursuit of artistic success

### CREATIVE PURSUIT

This ritual should involve the artistic pursuit for which you are calling on Athena, so take one of the tools you use, such as a pen, brush, or needle and thread, and produce a piece of art to dedicate to the goddess.

1 Write a poem, paint a watercolor, or embroider a tapestry, choosing a subject relevant to Athena herself—for example, an owl, an olive tree, or a goat. New clothing is also a symbol of Athena, as is the oak tree; or you might want to depict the goddess herself.

2 Once you have created your work of art, dedicate it to Athena, saying: "Athena, this is a gift for you. In return, please give me talent and success in my art."

3 Keep the work in the place where you practice your art so that you can look at it as you work. Whenever you feel inspiration or ability failing you, look at it and ask Athena for help.

GODDESS

# BASTET

*Egyptian goddess of fertility and protection*

Bastet is the Egyptian cat goddess, whose cult became so popular that it even eclipsed that of Isis. The Egyptians built a great temple to Bastet at Bubastis, which was set on an island surrounded by water except for the entrance passage. The shrine was 500 feet (150m) long and made of sparkling red granite set within an inner and an outer enclosure. Bastet is a protective goddess and is always gentle. However, when roused to anger she transforms into the lion goddess Sekhmut.

Bastet is often depicted as a cat, or as a woman with the head of a cat. Sometimes she is shown surrounded by kittens, and carrying a basket to put them in. She also carries a sistrum, a kind of rattle with four strings, which women used to scare off evil spirits. This is thought to be the origin of the traditional rhyme "Hey diddle diddle, the cat and the fiddle"; the cow jumping over the moon is the cow-headed moon goddess Hathor. Bastet is also associated with the moon, and is therefore a fertility goddess, since the moon governs the menstrual cycle.

Bastet became a focus for the witch hunts of the Middle Ages because of her association with women and the moon (along with Diana and a number of other goddesses). It was probably Bastet's link with cats that led to these animals being persecuted alongside women accused of witchcraft.

> *Nothing is so strong as gentleness, nothing so gentle as real strength.*

SAINT FRANCIS DE SALES

# RITUAL

## GENTLENESS

*Gentleness is a great virtue, especially when dealing with small children or animals that we do not want to intimidate. Bastet is strongly associated with cats, which symbolize her gentleness (by comparison with the fierceness of the lion, whose form Bastet takes when she is angry).*

### YOU WILL NEED

· Pens or paints
· A circle of tracing paper

**KINDNESS TO CATS**

One of the simplest ways to please Bastet is to show her special creatures care and compassion.

1 Start by spending some time around cats. If you have your own, this is very straightforward; if you do not, visit a friend or relative who has a cat, or simply make a point of stopping and petting any cats that you meet in the street.

2 When you are ready, draw or paint a cat on a circle of tracing paper. It does not matter how artistic you are; it is the effort and feeling you put into the drawing that counts.

3 When you have finished, tape the paper circle onto a window through which the moon will shine. The moonlight will bring Bastet's gentleness in through your window.

## RITUAL

# PROTECTION FROM NIGHTMARES

*Bastet protects her followers from evil spirits by shaking her sistrum (her sacred rattle). Since she is a moon goddess, she is especially powerful at dealing with night-time terrors. Use this ritual if you suffer from nightmares, or if anyone in your family does.*

### YOU WILL NEED

· A rattle

**NIGHT-TIME NOISE**

The ritual is at its strongest when performed during a full moon, but you can use it at any time when you feel the need, and then repeat it at each full moon.

-

You don't have to have a sistrum for this ritual, any kind of rattle will do.

1 Perform the ritual after dark, with the drapes or shutters open to the moon. Visit every room in the house in turn, shaking the rattle as you move around each room clockwise. Make sure you do not miss out any dark corners.

2 If you have a child who suffers from nightmares, get them to accompany you with their own rattle. You can turn it into a game if you like; the happier and noisier you both are, the better.

3 Finally, stand in the center of your bedroom and shake the rattle all around yourself. If you are performing the ritual with someone else, shake the rattles around each other.

*I have had dreams
and I have had nightmares,
but I have conquered
my nightmares because
of my dreams.*

JONAS SALK

# CHALCHIUHTLICUE

*Aztec goddess of water and fertility*

The Aztec wife of the rain god Tlaloc, Chalchiuhtlicue's name means "she whose skirt is made of jade." She is the goddess of fresh water, and rules over all the waters of the earth. She typifies the beauty of youth. She is also a fertility goddess (crops need water to grow, after all), and is frequently associated with marriage. The Aztecs often invoked her to protect their newborn babies.

According to the Aztecs, there were thirteen world ages; Chalchiuhtlicue resided over the fourth age (we are now in the fifth age). She gave birth to the Tlalocs, rain gods who lived in the hills, and she has the ability to create natural phenomena such as hurricanes and whirlpools, and to cause death by drowning. She ended the fourth age by releasing a deluge to punish the wicked; the only survivors were those who had the ability to turn themselves into fish.

Chalchiuhtlicue is the guardian of young women, being young and beautiful herself. She usually wears a dress made of jade, often covered in waterlilies, and frequently wears a string of precious stones around her neck. Since she is a fertility goddess, she is also associated with fruit and vegetation, and is sometimes symbolized as a river with a prickly pear tree growing from it, which in turn symbolizes the human heart.

# MARRIAGE

*This ritual will bring Chalchiuhtlicue's blessing for a long and happy marriage, and should be performed a day or two before your wedding. At the end of the ritual you will have an object to keep for as long as your marriage lasts, symbolizing the goddess's blessing on your partnership.*

## YOU WILL NEED

‣ An offering associated with Chalchiuhtlicue

### PLEASING THE GODDESS

Choose an offering associated with Chalchiuhtlicue, such as fruit, waterlilies, or something made of jade.

-

Perform this ritual at a place with a natural water source, such as by a stream, river, pond, or even the sea.

1 Take the offering to a source of natural water. Cast it into the water and watch as it disappears from sight.

2 Now look around until you find a natural object that catches your eye, and that you can take home as a keepsake. It might be a pebble, a shell, or a piece of driftwood. It should be something that will last, and that will not crumble away or rot. If you empty your mind, you should find yourself drawn to an object.

3 Take the object home with you and keep it somewhere safe.

4 To ensure an open and trusting marriage, tell your partner about the ritual, and keep the object in a shared place.

## RITUAL

# PROTECTING NEWBORN BABIES

*As the Aztecs did, you can call on Chalchiuhtlicue to protect your newborn baby, by carrying out this ritual before the birth.*

## YOU WILL NEED

- A jade talisman of your choosing
- A drawstring pouch

### PROTECTIVE TALISMAN

Jade is the symbolic stone of Chalchiuhtlicue. The talisman you choose could be an earring, a small carved object, or simply an unmounted stone.

-

Choose a drawstring pouch made from a natural material, such as leather, velvet, cotton, or linen.

1 Hold the jade object in your hands and say to Chalchiuhtlicue: "I ask you to fill this jade stone with your spirit to protect _____ in the first few months of life." If you don't yet know the child's name, say: "to protect the child of _____ and _____ in the first few months of life."

2 Now place the stone inside the drawstring pouch, and secure it underneath the mattress or crib, making sure of course that the baby cannot reach it.

3 Leave the talisman in place until the baby has moved on from its first crib, then remove the stone and keep it as a memento.

GODDESS

# DIANA

## *Roman goddess of the hunt and the moon*

The chaste Roman goddess Diana is the guardian of virginity. She also protects women in childbirth. Diana lives in the woodlands and forests, and is often depicted carrying a bow and arrow. Her cult center was at Ephesus, where she displaced her Greek counterpart, Artemis. The statues of Diana at Ephesus depict her as a many-breasted goddess, because in her earliest form she was said to suckle all the wild animals.

Diana is the sister of the sun god Apollo and, as his feminine counterpart, is therefore associated with the moon. She is often represented with a cat (an almost universal symbol of the moon and of femininity), so she was considered a leader of witches in the Middle Ages.

One myth tells the story of how Diana went to bathe in a woodland pool. She undressed and handed her bow, arrows, and clothes to her nymphs. A young prince, Actaeon, arrived in the woods with his friends and his hounds, ready for stag hunting the next day. He chanced upon the pool, and saw the goddess bathing naked. Diana was so angry that she turned Actaeon into a stag, whereupon he was pursued and torn to pieces by his own dogs.

## RITUAL

# CHASTITY

*Many of us go through periods in our lives when we feel the need to abstain from sexual activity. Perhaps this is so that we can focus all our energy elsewhere, or to bring some calm and balance into a difficult love life. However, it can be hard to maintain our resolve. This ritual calls on the virgin goddess Diana to help.*

### YOU WILL NEED

· Four white candles
· Five white lilies
· Clean white clothes

**PEACEFUL BATHING**
For this ritual you need to find a quiet time to take a bath.

1 Run a bath and place a candle and a lily at each corner of the bath, saving the fifth lily for Stage 3.

2 Light the candles and switch off any other lights.

3 Remove the petals from the remaining lily and scatter them on top of the water. As you remove each petal, say: "I call on you, Diana, to preserve my chastity." As you remove the final petal, say: "Preserve my chastity until I am ready to relinquish it."

4 Get into the bath and, as you wash, imagine that you are washing away all sexual thoughts and desires.

5 When you get out of the bath, dress in clean white clothes, and spend the rest of the evening alone.

## RITUAL

# CHILDBIRTH

*Childbirth is a deeply mystical and important event, but many of us approach this time with trepidation. The mother's body experiences momentous upheaval, and although the process of having a child is safer in this modern age than ever before, we can still benefit from some reassurance by invoking Diana, the patron goddess of women in childbirth.*

## YOU WILL NEED

- A snipping of cat's hair, black if possible
- A small pouch or locket
- Playlist or CD of woodland sounds

### PROTECTIVE CHOICES

Cats are sacred to Diana. If you can't find fur from a black cat, any color will suffice. It is also preferable to use fur from a female cat that has not been sterilized, though again, this is not essential.

-

Choose a pouch or locket that you will be happy wearing during the birth. For example, you might prefer a locket on a bracelet to one that you wear around your neck, or perhaps even an ankle chain.

1 Put the snipping of cat's fur into a small pouch or locket, and keep it near you throughout your pregnancy as a good-luck amulet.

2 During the birth, wear the amulet, and play a soundtrack of woodland sounds to invoke the spirit of Diana, so that she will be present at the birth to keep you safe.

# EPONA

*Celtic-Roman goddess of healing, fertility, and animals*

Epona accompanies the soul on its final journey, beyond death. She began as a Celtic horse goddess, whose center of worship was in Gaul. Her association with the horse made her a patron goddess of domestic animals, especially dogs and birds; through her function of protecting and nurturing them, she also became a goddess of healing and fertility. Epona is usually depicted on horseback, often surrounded by horses, fruit, ears of corn, and a cornucopia, or horn of plenty, which is her symbol.

The Celts also associated Epona with sacred waters, and many of her shrines are situated close to thermal springs. Perhaps for this reason she sometimes appears naked, like a water nymph, and was occasionally seen as a patron goddess of springs, streams, and rivers.

When the Romans conquered Gaul they instantly took to Epona, and the cavalry adopted her as their patroness. They built shrines to her in their stables, which they decorated with roses. Epona was the only Celtic goddess to be given her own temple in Rome, and even her own festival (on December 18th). Through the Roman army, the worship of Epona spread across the Roman Empire, and survived its fall. She was worshipped right through until the 12th century.

# HEALING

*Epona is the goddess of healing, and for this ritual you will visualize her unburdening you of your illness, or that of someone you know.*

## YOU WILL NEED

- Pen and paper
- White ribbon

1 Compose a four- or five-word expression of the healing you want Epona to bring about, for you or someone else.

2 Write this down in the center of a sheet of paper, and roll the paper up into a scroll.

3 Close your eyes and chant the words you have written. As you do so, visualize yourself standing in a green valley: in one hand you hold the scroll, and in the other a black velvet pouch. In front of you is a steep hill, and as you

watch, a horse and rider appear on the brow of the hill. As they come down the hill toward you, you recognize Epona. When she reaches you, she takes the black pouch from your hand.

4 Still chanting, visualize Epona starting to ride up the hill behind you. You realize that the black pouch contains the illness, and you watch as she takes it away up the hill, faster and faster, until she, and the sickness, disappear over the horizon.

**FORWARD PLANNING**
Read through the whole ritual and make sure you understand what it is you should be visualizing, before you close your eyes.

5 Stop chanting and open your eyes. Tie the scroll with a white ribbon and put it somewhere safe until the sickness has passed.

# RITUAL

## CARING FOR ANIMALS

*Epona is the champion of animals, and especially domestic animals. As a goddess of healing, she is especially ready to help heal animals that are unwell or neglected, whether it is your pet cat or an injured bird found lying on the ground.*

### YOU WILL NEED

- An iron horseshoe
- A white rose

**POINT OF FOCUS**

An animal's bed, cage, or sleeping area is the center of its territory, and represents its sense of security, so this ritual focuses on the place where it usually sleeps.

-

This ritual uses a horseshoe as a symbol of the horse goddess, and a white rose because white is the color of healing.

1 Hang the horseshoe above the animal's bed, either on the wall or from a cord, or perhaps stand it on a shelf above the bed. The horseshoe must be the right way up—that is, in a "U" shape, so that it is cupped to hold the blessing of Epona.

2 Take the white rose and remove the petals from it. Hold these in your hands, close your eyes, and imagine Epona gently blowing her blessing on them.

3 Now place them in the animal's bed and leave them there until it has recovered.

4 When the animal has returned to good health, take the petals outside and scatter them on the earth.

# EZILI

*Haitian Vodou goddess of love and beauty*

---

Ezili, also known as Ezili Freda, is both the bringer of good health and prosperity, and the harbinger of discord and envy. She is a glamorous figure, sweetly scented and beautifully dressed, living in great luxury and spending much of her time beautifying herself. She is fond of flowers, jewelry, rich clothing, and fine perfumes, and has a particular weakness for sweet desserts.

Each Vodou spirit has a Catholic counterpart, and Ezili's is the Virgin Mary, who is said to have appeared on top of a palm tree near a small town in Haiti called Ville Bonheur. Pilgrims began leaving small offerings of food at the base of the tree for Ezili; now that the tree is gone, pilgrims visit the waterfalls nearby to bathe in the blessed waters. Ezili's symbol is a heart pierced by a jewel-encrusted dagger.

Ezili is generous in her role as a love goddess. She has three principal lovers among the Vodou gods, but also undertakes mystical marriages with mortals. During Vodou ceremonies, Ezili possesses her followers as they dance, so that they move seductively and sometimes wantonly. She also has a demanding and jealous streak, sometimes sitting with her knees drawn up to her chest and her fists clenched, weeping for lost love and for the shortness of life.

*So she thoroughly taught him that one cannot take pleasure without giving pleasure, and that every gesture, every caress, every touch, every glance, every last bit of the body has its secret, which brings happiness to the person who knows how to wake it.*

HERMANN HESSE, *SIDDHARTHA*

## SEXUAL LOVE

*However strong our sexual relationship is with our partner, there are always times when it flags a little for one reason or another. During such times, perform this ritual with your partner to invoke Ezili's help.*

### YOU WILL NEED

- Candles
- Scented oils or body moisturizer
- Colorful, seductive clothing and jewelry
- Music that you find seductive

1 Like Ezili, you should be perfumed, so have a scented, candlelit bath, then use oils or body moisturizer to perfume your skin. As you smooth the cream or oil into your skin, close your eyes and ask Ezili to be within you. While you are preparing yourself, your partner should do likewise.

2 Dress in colorful, glamorous, seductive clothing and jewelry.

3 At a prearranged time, meet your partner in a candlelit room in the house, where you play music and dance. Put on the sexiest, most seductive music you can find, and start dancing sensually together, moving your bodies closely but not touching.

4 Gradually progress to stroking each other as you dance, perhaps even undoing the occasional button or fastening. Take things as slowly as you can, and continue dancing until you have all but forgotten the music and are making love.

### DATE NIGHT

Set aside an entire evening for the ritual. You need to begin early, by preparing yourself for a passionate encounter with your partner.

> *If we had no winter, the spring would not be so pleasant: if we did not sometimes taste of adversity, prosperity would not be so welcome.*

ANNE BRADSTREET,
*MEDITATIONS DIVINE AND MORAL*

## RITUAL

# PROSPERITY

*Ezili has the power to bestow prosperity, and this ritual is designed to invoke her to bring you wealth.*

### YOU WILL NEED

- Several candles of different colors, or multicolored candles
- Five copper or gold coins
- Five silver coins
- Two small pouches or containers
- A larger pouch or container into which the first two will fit

> **VODOU INSPIRATION**
>
> When it comes to choosing colors for your candles, avoid black or white, and bear in mind that pink and pale blue are Ezili's favorite colors.
>
> -
>
> Followers of Haitian Vodou use everyday, modern objects for their rituals, so you can do likewise. For example, you can use commercial packaging to hold the coins for this ritual, but bear in mind that it needs to be weatherproof.

1 Light the candles.

2 Standing in front of the candles, place the five copper or gold coins in one small container and the five silver coins in the other.

3 Place both small containers inside the larger one. As you do so, invoke the goddess by saying: "Ezili, as I bring these coins together, make them multiply even further."

4 Close the larger container and hang it outside the highest window in your home, where her goddess energy can fill it. Leave it hanging until you have acquired the wealth you desire.

# FRIGGA

*Scandinavian goddess of fertility, love, and the sky*

The wife of the supreme Norse god Odin, Frigga is the Scandinavians' most important mother goddess. She sometimes protects warriors from her husband, and makes men fruitful in marriage. Although Frigga is the patron of marriage and motherhood, she is often unfaithful, even with her husband's brothers. The word "Friday" is a corruption, through the German, of "Frigga's day."

Frigga is depicted as tall and elegant, usually with a bunch of keys hanging from her belt. She often wears long robes that she can make light or dark at will. She lives in her own hall at Asgard (the home of the Scandinavian gods), which was known as Fensalir, meaning "hall of water." She is also goddess of the sky, and she and her eleven handmaidens weave multicolored clouds. Her messenger, Gna, rides through the sky on horseback.

Frigga knows everyone's fate, but she will not disclose it and cannot alter it. However, she did try to change her son Balder's destiny. Balder dreamt that his life was in danger, so Frigga extracted a solemn oath from every living thing that it would not harm her son. However, she did not ask the mistletoe, and her son was killed by an arrow made of mistletoe wood, and exiled to the underworld.

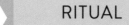

# RITUAL

## GOOD FORTUNE

*Frigga is usually depicted wearing a bunch of keys on her belt, so this ritual uses a key to symbolize her.*

### YOU WILL NEED

· An old key

**LOCKLESS KEY**
You will need a key that you do not have a lock for—perhaps from a previous house, or an old one you have found in a secondhand store. Choose one made of a shiny metal such as steel or brass, rather than a dull one such as iron.

1 Clean and polish the key as much as possible so that it is bright and shiny.

2 Stand just inside your front door, facing into the house, and hold the key out in front of you. Say: "Frigga, put your good fortune in this key so that it will always bless me."

3 Walk around each room in your house, holding the key out in front of you as you do so. Touch any special objects in your home with the key, such as your bed for fortune in your relationships, your telephone for fortune with your friends, your computer for fortune in your work or study, and so on.

4 When you have completed the ritual, hang the key from a hook over the front door, and always keep it clean and shiny.

# RITUAL

## PROTECTION FROM DANGER

*This ritual will invoke Frigga's protection on you all
year round.*

### YOU WILL NEED

· A flowerbed, plant pot,
  or window box
· Seeds

1 Carefully dig the soil in the area to be planted,
making sure it is free from weeds.

2 Sow the seeds in the shape of the Nordic rune for
protection (like a capital "Y" but with the central
upstroke continued up to the top, so that the symbol
has three prongs pointing upward). As you sprinkle
the seeds on the ground, say to Frigga: "As these seeds
grow tall and strong, protect me (or us) for the whole
year long."

3 Look after your seedlings carefully, thinning and
weeding any that grow outside the rune shape.
Eventually the plants may grow too bushy to see the
shape clearly, but it will still be there.

4 At the end of the fall, collect some seeds so that
you can repeat the ritual the following year, but
do not dig up the plants until you are ready to re-sow
in the spring.

### PLANTING SPACE

The ritual entails planting
seeds in your yard, or in a
window box or plant pot
if you do not have a yard.

GODDESS

# GAIA

*Greek goddess of nature, marriage, and oaths*

---

Gaia is the primordial creator goddess of the Greeks, whose name means "earth." She was born from Chaos (one of the infernal deities), along with Eros, the god of desire. She is the mother of the twelve giant Titans, who between them gave rise to most of the gods and goddesses of the Greek pantheon. She had an oracle at Delphi before Apollo did, where she answered people's questions (cryptically) through her priestesses.

Gaia resented the tyranny of her husband and son Ouranos, who made her keep all her children inside her for fear that they would be more powerful than him. So she gave a sickle to her son Kronos to dismember Ouranos while she was mating with him. This separated the earth (Gaia) and the sky (Ouranos) permanently. When Kronos later turned out to be just as bad as Ouranos, Gaia helped to protect his son Zeus from him by hiding Zeus on the island of Crete.

Gaia is gentle and nurturing; in some versions of Greek mythology she is also the originator of humans. Certainly she is a great fertility goddess who brings life to the corn and the fruits of the earth. As well as being the ultimate nature goddess, she also presides over marriages and oaths.

## RITUAL

# EMPATHY WITH NATURE

*This ritual is best performed in late summer, at harvest time, and will help put you more in tune with the earth's cycles.*

### YOU WILL NEED

· Fruits and vegetables
· Other organic,
  simple foodstuffs

1 Harvest foods such as fruit and vegetables that you have grown yourself, or go into the countryside and collect berries, nuts, and fruits. If you must buy the food, choose only organic fruit and vegetables, and no processed foods.

2 Cook the harvested foods very simply, if at all, so that their taste is not sullied.

3 Ideally, picnic outside on uncooked vegetables, fruits, nuts, organic bread, and perhaps organic honey. Better still, have a party and invite other people to join in your harvest celebration.

4 Whatever you eat, save one-tenth of it as an offering to Gaia, to thank her for the fruits of the earth.

5 Scoop out a hollow in the ground, and place your offering in it. Cover the food with leaves, then cover the whole area with earth again.

### GOOD FOOD

Gaia gives us the natural fruits of the earth, and brings life and fertility to the crops, so this ritual involves spending the day eating only freshly harvested, organic foods.

## OATHS

*You can use this ritual to strengthen your resolve to honor an oath, and to make it more binding. Since Gaia also presides over marriages, this is a particularly good ritual for swearing a marriage oath.*

### YOU WILL NEED

· Soil
· An earthenware, stone, or clay bowl
· Two black candles
· Rosemary plant

**SINGLE OR SHARED OATHS**

You can choose to swear an oath to yourself, or make a shared oath, such as an oath of trust or fidelity.

-

Choose a bowl that is as natural as possible—in other words, unglazed and simple in design. Black candles are used to signify the solemnity of the ritual, and rosemary for remembrance.

1 Take a handful of fresh soil and place it in the bowl, then stand the bowl of earth on a table with a black candle on either side of it.

2 To swear the oath, place your hand in the bowl and say: "I swear by Gaia and by the earth I walk on that ..." and then specify the oath you are swearing. If you are swearing a joint oath with another person, you should both place your hands in the bowl together.

3 Sprinkle the earth in the yard—or in a plant pot—and grow a rosemary plant in it. Rosemary signifies remembrance, so that you never forget your promise.

# HATHOR

*Egyptian goddess of love, fertility, music, and dance*

The Egyptian mother goddess, and also the goddess of love, Hathor is most often depicted as a cow, or as a woman holding the sun between two cow's horns on her head. Her hair is often styled into the shape of an "omega" symbol, and she is sometimes depicted browsing among papyrus reeds.

Hathor is a very important deity, concerned with sexual love, fertility, and erotic music and dancing. She is the daughter of Ra (the sun god) and the consort of Horus (the sky god), and was closely associated with the Egyptian royal family: all princesses automatically became her priestesses, and pharaohs were known as "sons of Hathor." She is often shown suckling the pharaoh Amenhotep II.

Hathor originally lived in Nubia, where she was a wild lioness, but Ra sent for her to come and live in Egypt. There she lost her feral nature to become elegant and charming. However, she was capable of returning to her former leonine style. For instance, Ra once sent her to wreak destruction on the earth to punish the people for suggesting he was too old to rule. Hathor was so bloodthirsty that Ra was obliged to find a way of stopping her from destroying everyone. He flooded the fields with ale dyed red and, thinking it was blood, Hathor drank it greedily until she became too intoxicated to continue wreaking havoc. It must be said, however, that this was a rare departure from her usual benign nature.

# GUARDING CHILDREN'S FUTURE

*This ritual invokes Hathor's blessing on a child throughout its life. As a mother goddess, and also a cow goddess, Hathor is strongly associated with milk, and by blessing the milk that the baby drinks, you can nourish the child in both a physical and spiritual sense.*

## YOU WILL NEED

- Sandalwood incense
- A rock crystal
- Thread or string
- A child's rattle

### EXTENDED BENEFITS

The rock crystal is a stone of protection that will guard over the child as it grows, and brings peaceful sleep, a valuable by-product of this ritual. Sandalwood is used because it is sacred to Hathor.

1 Light the incense (not too close to the baby), and tie the rock crystal securely with a piece of thread or string.

2 Hang the crystal above the baby's head while it drinks its milk (if this is difficult to do, ask someone else to hold the crystal).

3 Allow the crystal to swing gently in clockwise circles. As it does so, call on Hathor, saying: "Hathor, nourish this child with your blessing as he/she grows into a man/woman."

4 The rattle is another traditional symbol of Hathor, and is shaken to drive away evil spirits. Bless your child's rattle by holding it and saying: "Hathor, give this rattle power to drive away evil and harm."

## RITUAL

## FOREIGN TRAVEL

*Hathor did not come from Egypt originally, but from Nubia. Since she was a foreign goddess, the Egyptians associated her with travel in foreign parts, and asked for her blessing before embarking on journeys abroad. So whether you are traveling for work or on vacation, you can ask Hathor to protect you when you go abroad.*

### YOU WILL NEED

· A memento from home

**SPECIAL KEEPSAKE**

Choose a memento that will remind you of home and that you can carry with you easily. It might be a pressed flower from your yard, a piece of furnishing fabric from your favorite room, or perhaps a special teaspoon or even a swatch of paint. Choose something that belongs in the house or yard, and that means something special to you.

1 On the morning of your departure, find a quiet moment and take the chosen object in your hand, saying the following words: "Hathor, as I travel, I shall carry a piece of my home. Let me enjoy my journey, but bring me safely back."

2 Pack your memento somewhere safe in your luggage. If you feel homesick at any time, take it out and hold it, and ask Hathor to renew your enthusiasm for your journey.

# HEL

### *Norse goddess of the underworld*

The Norse goddess of the underworld, or Nifleim, Hel is responsible for those who die of sickness or old age. She is cold, but she is not cruel. She is frightening to look at, since half her face is human and the other half is either blank or grossly distorted. She has the body of a living woman, but the legs of a moldering corpse. Her name is the source of the word "hell."

Hel is the youngest child of the evil god Loki and the giantess Angrboda. She is sister to the Midgard worm, who will eventually flood the earth by lashing the sea with its tail; and also to Fenrir, the ghostly wolf who will one day swallow the sun at Ragnarok, the last battle, which will bring about the end of the world.

When the goddess Frigga's son Balder was killed by Loki's trickery, he was delivered to Hel's underworld. The gods all begged Hel to return Balder to them, but she refused. Eventually, however, they showed such sorrow that even Hel was moved. She agreed to return Balder on one condition: that every creature in the world, without exception, must weep for him. They all did apart from Loki, who refused—which is why Balder was not released but condemned to remain in Nifleim until the end of the world.

*I know that in life there will be sickness, devastation, disappointments, heartache— it's a given. What's not a given is the way you choose to get through it all. If you look hard enough, you can always find the bright side.*

**RASHIDA JONES**

# RITUAL

## EASING SICKNESS

*This ritual calls on Hel to ease the suffering of long-term illness. This may be a chronic condition such as arthritis, impaired vision, or eczema. Hel is not the warmest or gentlest of goddesses, but she is not without emotion: she will listen when you call on her.*

### YOU WILL NEED

· An orange candle
· A black veil, such as a chiffon scarf or some similar material

**GAIN SOME RELIEF**
Orange is the color of health and vigor, so this ritual uses an orange candle.

-

It is best to repeat this ritual at each full moon, but you can also use it in between if you feel the need.

1 Light the orange candle in a darkened room, and stand or sit in front of it.

2 Drape the black veil over your head so that it covers one half of your face. Now say: "Hel, I invoke you to help me in my sickness and to ease my suffering" (or use someone else's name if the ritual is on their behalf).

3 Close your eyes and spend a few moments imagining the flame of the candle growing larger and burning away the pain and suffering.

# BEREAVEMENT

*This ritual can help you to cope with a bereavement and the grieving process.*

## YOU WILL NEED

- A small candle
- A fireproof black-and-white or gray bowl
- A memento of the person for whom you are grieving
- Pen and paper

### REACHING OUT

Choose a bowl that is black and white or gray to symbolize both the positive and the negative aspects of death, the opposing characteristics of Hel herself.

–

For the memento, choose something that the person used to wear in contact with the skin, such as some fabric from a favorite piece of clothing, a ring, or a pair of spectacles.

1 Light the candle in the bowl, and place the memento on the table beside it.

2 Imagine that you have the opportunity to say one thing to the person you are grieving for. Write this on the paper—try to keep it to just a line or two, so that it is clear and focused.

3 Holding the memento in your hand, burn the paper in the flame. As you watch it burn, imagine the words disappearing from your view and being taken by Hel to deliver to your loved one.

4 Keep the memento with you—around your neck, in your bag, on your desk, or wherever you want it—until you feel ready to put it away.

> *It is a curious thing, the death of a loved one. ... It is like walking up the stairs to your bedroom in the dark, and thinking there is one more stair than there is. Your foot falls down, through the air, and there is a sickly moment of dark surprise as you try and readjust the way you thought of things.*

**LEMONY SNICKET,**
*HORSERADISH: BITTER TRUTHS YOU CAN'T AVOID*

GODDESS

# HERA

*Greek goddess of marriage and childbirth*

Hera is the queen of the Greek goddesses, the wife and sister of Zeus. She and Zeus have three children: the smith god Hephaestus; the god of war, Ares; and the goddess of youth, Hebe. According to many versions, Hera conceived these children alone, either by slapping her hand on the ground or by eating lettuce; whichever it was, they were born out of hatred rather than love, and she shows them little affection.

Hera is a particularly angry goddess, though arguably with good reason, since she has to put up with Zeus' many infidelities. As a result she is deeply jealous, and pursues his lovers and the children they conceive with hatred and vengeance: she put serpents in Heracles' cradle, drove the foster parents of Dionysus mad, and set Io under the guard of a giant monster. She also tried to prevent the birth of Artemis and Apollo.

Hera is a majestic figure, often depicted wearing a diadem and veil. Her chariot is pulled by peacocks, which are her sacred animals, as are the cow and the crow. The pomegranate, a symbol of marriage, is also sacred to her. In one legend, Hera appeared to the hero Jason as a withered hag, requesting that he carry her over a raging torrent. Despite her hideous appearance, Jason did so. In return, Hera enlisted the aid of Athena and Aphrodite to help Jason during his voyage in search of the Golden Fleece.

# RITUAL

## PROTECTION FROM INFIDELITY

*Most of us enter relationships believing that we can trust our partner to be faithful. Sadly, not everyone continues to feel as confident. If you are concerned that your partner may be unfaithful—or simply may be tempted—you can call on Hera to help you.*

### YOU WILL NEED

· A pomegranate

**SACRED FRUIT**

The pomegranate, the symbol of marriage, is sacred to Hera, so is used for this ritual.

1 Sit at a table and cut a pomegranate in half, then remove and save the seeds, and eat the flesh. As you do so, reflect on what you can reasonably expect from your partner in your relationship, and on what they can expect from you in return.

2 When you have finished eating, take three of the seeds and clean them thoroughly; you can discard the rest.

3 Go to the bedroom you share with your partner, and place the seeds on the pillow of the bed. Call on Hera, saying: "Hera, as the pomegranate protects its seeds, so I ask you to protect me. Keep this relationship free from temptation and infidelity."

4 Then take the seeds from the pillow and place them under the mattress on your partner's side of the bed.

## RITUAL

# STRENGTH IN TIMES OF CONFLICT

*Hera often finds herself in conflict, particularly with her husband Zeus, and is frequently upset and angry. However, she always maintains her strength; she never wavers or gives in. Use this ritual to help you emulate Hera's strength in times of conflict.*

### YOU WILL NEED

· A peacock feather

**SAFE SPACE**
Find a place where you feel completely safe and private, and therefore able to be strong without any danger of further conflict. This might be in your bedroom, in the bathroom with the door locked, or while out walking.

1 Hold the peacock feather, look at it, and turn it around in your hand; notice that it is straight, tall, and strong.

2 Meditate on the feather, and consider how it resembles the qualities you would like to display. You might find inspiration in its shape, its color, the feel of it, the quill.

3 Keep the feather in a safe place. Whenever you feel your strength waning, take out the feather and remember what it represents to you, the qualities it stands for. As you look at it, invoke Hera with the words: "Hera, lend me your strength to cope with my difficulties."

# ISHTAR

*Mesopotamian goddess of sexual love, fertility, and war*

Ishtar was worshipped for over two-and-a-half thousand years, from around 2500 B.C. In most traditions she is the daughter of the moon god, Sin. Although she is a passionately sexual goddess, she is always a virgin: this is because she periodically regains her virginity by rebathing in a sacred lake. Ishtar is symbolized by an eight-pointed star, and her sacred beast is the lion. The goddess is often depicted with wings, and carrying a double-headed mace decorated with lion heads.

Ishtar is easily roused to terrifying anger. She is the patron goddess of harlots and takes many lovers—but every man who falls in love with Ishtar dies. She tried to seduce the hero Gilgamesh, but he refused, realizing that he would perish if he became her lover. This made Ishtar so angry that she released the Bull of Heaven against him, and although Gilgamesh managed to kill the bull, the penalty for this—as Ishtar knew—was punishment by the gods, who caused his greatest friend, Enkidu, to die.

This story is typical of Ishtar's vengeful nature when slighted, and yet she is also capable of great love. She loved her husband Tammuz so much that she descended into the underworld to rescue him when he died.

## RITUAL

## SEXUAL PASSION

*Ishtar was not afraid to express her deep sexual passions, but many of us find it hard at times to be open about our sexuality. Use this ritual to call on Ishtar to help you express your sexual self openly and honestly.*

### YOU WILL NEED

· A bowl of rosewater

**VISUALIZATION**

Make sure you have read through the whole ritual, and understand what you should be visualizing, before you close your eyes.

1 In the bedroom, remove all of your clothes and put the bowl of rosewater next to the bed. Lie on the bed and close your eyes.

2 Breathe deeply until you are relaxed, then imagine a ball of golden light ahead of you. As it moves toward you, watch as it turns into a golden lion.

3 Stroke the lion, and sink your fingers deep into its fur. Enjoy the feel and the smell of it. Sink deeper into the lion's fur until you merge with it.

4 Slowly open your eyes.

5 Rise from the bed, dip your finger in the rosewater, and trace an eight-pointed star between your breasts. Throughout the day, touch this part of your body and feel the passion of the lion enveloping you once again.

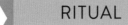

## RITUAL

# FAITHFULNESS

*Although Ishtar was not sexually faithful to her husband Tammuz, her love for him was so true that she literally braved hell to be with him. Her faithfulness in love was strong and deep, and this ritual asks for her steadfastness for you and your loved one.*

## YOU WILL NEED

· Something intimate belonging to your partner, matched by something of your own
· A small box into which these items will fit
· Enough red ribbon to wrap around the box seven times, plus a little extra

### SPECIAL CLOSENESS

To perform this ritual you will need something intimate belonging to your partner, such as a lock of hair or a well-worn item of clothing. After acquiring this intimate belonging, match it with something similar of your own—a lock of your hair, or a piece of clothing.

1 Take the two intimate items and tie them together with a small piece of ribbon, then put them into the box. Now take the remaining ribbon and cut it into seven pieces, each long enough to tie once around the box.

2 Wrap each length of ribbon carefully around the box, and as you tie each one, say: "Hold us together with the bond of faithfulness."

3 Repeat this until the box is bound by all seven pieces of ribbon. Keep the box in a safe place, and don't allow the ribbons to become dislodged or untied.

# ISIS

*Egyptian goddess of life, fertility, and magic*

Isis represents all the best aspects of womanhood: love, loyalty, protection, motherhood, and sexuality. She is also very skilled in magic. She is the wife of Osiris, who is also her brother, and like the goddess Hathor, is often represented wearing a crown of cow's horns enclosing a sun disk.

Isis obtained her power by magically creating a serpent. She put this serpent in the path of the sun god Ra, and it bit him. She told Ra that she could cure him, but only on condition that he told her his secret name. Eventually, as the poison took hold, Ra realized he had no choice, so he told her. With this secret knowledge, Isis was able to appropriate a portion of Ra's power for herself.

Osiris was killed by his brother Seth, who shut Osiris in a coffer and cast it adrift in the Nile. Isis searched everywhere for the coffer, and eventually recovered it and brought it home. Seth was so angry that he dismembered the body and scattered the pieces across Egypt. Isis dutifully recovered every piece apart from his genitals, which she could not find, so she made him an artificial phallus. She embalmed and bandaged her husband's body—the first ever mummification—then used her magic powers to breathe life back into him.

*Loyalty and friendship,*
*which is to me the same,*
*created all the wealth that*
*I've ever thought I'd have.*

—

**ERNIE BANKS**

# RITUAL

## LOYALTY

*You can use this ritual to call on Isis to strengthen your own loyalty if you feel tempted to betray a trust, or to engender loyalty in someone else.*

### YOU WILL NEED

· A tall white candle
· A garnet, unmounted or in a piece of jewelry

**EARLY START**

This ritual should be performed in the morning, as soon as you wake up if possible. You will need a garnet, the precious stone that symbolizes loyalty.

1 Light a tall, white candle and stand in front of it. Hold the garnet in front of the candle so that it sparkles in the light of the flame.

2 As you watch the light shining on and through the garnet, think about the matter in which you want to strengthen your sense of loyalty.

3 Imagine yourself, or whoever is concerned, in a situation that presents the opportunity to break trust. Imagine yourself, or the person concerned, resisting it. You might, for example, visualize a situation in which a friend asks you to tell them a secret, but you resist, saying: "No, I can't tell you that."

4 Now put the garnet in your pocket, or wear it if it is a piece of jewelry, and keep it with you until you are confident that the threat of disloyalty has passed.

## RITUAL

# PREGNANCY

*Isis is sometimes symbolized as a cow, or depicted wearing a cow's horns.*
*Since cows produce milk, deeply linked with pregnancy and motherhood,*
*it is appropriate that this ritual uses milk to call on Isis' blessing.*
*Moreover, the more natural the milk you use, the better; use full-fat,*
*organic milk if you can.*

## YOU WILL NEED

· Full-fat, organic milk
· Round, gold-colored disk

### FINDING A SUN DISK

You will need something round, flat, and gold to represent
Isis' sun disk. You might have something made of real gold,
such as a pendant, but if not, you can improvise. A pet-collar
tag is a possibility, or perhaps a metal lid from a container;
you might even have a small piece of gold foil.

1 Pour a glass of milk and drop your sun disk into it.

2 Dip a finger into the milk, and place a single drop on each of your breasts and on your stomach. As you do so, invoke Isis, saying: "Isis, keep this child safe inside me, and keep me safe to protect it. Bless it in the womb and bless it in the world."

3 When you have finished the invocation, drink the milk and visualize Isis' blessing coursing through you and your child.

# RITUAL

## MOTHERHOOD

*For this ritual you will build a shrine to Isis somewhere in your house, perhaps on a table, in an alcove, or on a windowsill.*

### YOU WILL NEED

· A symbol for each of the four elements (see Stage 1)
· A symbol of the moon (see Stage 2)
· Symbols of your children (see Stage 3)

**SHRINE FOR SUPPORT**

The shrine represents the holistic nature of motherhood, when you might be called upon to provide anything for your children—from spiritual refuge and moral education to clean socks or a lift to the train station.

1 You need to symbolize each of the four elements in your shrine: a clay bowl filled with sand to represent earth, a glass bowl filled with rain or spring water, a candle in a brass or gold candlestick for fire, and an empty glass for air.

2 Add something to represent the moon, too, as this is the symbol of fertility and motherhood; you might use a round mirror or a glass orb.

3 If you wish, add an object of your choice to represent each of your children, such as a swatch of clothing.

4 Keep the shrine clean, and refresh the water regularly.

5 Whenever you feel in need of support as a mother, stand at your shrine, light the candle, and silently ask Isis to lend you some of her strength. Meditate on your own strength and love as a mother.

GODDESS

# KUAN YIN

*Chinese goddess of mercy, compassion, and newlyweds*

Kuan Yin is a motherly figure. She is said to bestow children on the faithful, and newly married couples often ask her to bless them in this way. She frequently shares influence with the Queen of Heaven, Tin Hau, and sometimes takes one of Tin Hau's titles: Goddess of the Southern Sea.

Kuan Yin is often depicted with a lotus flower, holding a jar containing the dew of compassion in one hand and a branch of willow in the other. She has an attendant, Lung Nu, who carries other objects such as her pearls. She is frequently depicted wearing a white veil and holding a child, and is sometimes shown as a thousand-armed, thousand-eyed goddess.

Kuan Yin, originally an Indian princess, was a Buddhist bodhisattva: a mortal who has achieved enlightenment and earned the right to enter Nirvana—the place of liberated souls—but who chooses instead to remain on earth and help others become enlightened. As she reached the gates of heaven, Kuan Yin heard someone on earth cry and so turned back, vowing that she would stay on earth to do all she could to help ease suffering. She will not enter heaven until everyone on earth has become enlightened and can go there with her. She is often invoked in times of danger.

## RITUAL

# COMPASSION

*Kuan Yin has infinite compassion for everyone. We can become inured to suffering if we are not in direct contact with it, largely because the media inundates our senses with so many accounts of human tragedy. This ritual helps us to regain some of Kuan Yin's compassion for all people, not only for our loved ones.*

### YOU WILL NEED

· A bowl of spring or rainwater
· A willow branch

**1** Sit cross-legged, holding the bowl of water in one hand and the willow in the other.

**2** Think about the meaning and value of the compassion you wish to regain. Meditate on what it is that you would like to be able to feel, and why.

**3** Spend a few minutes appreciating the quality that Kuan Yin has, and why you want to share it.

**4** Now imagine all your hard-headedness and selfishness being drained out of you by Kuan Yin.

**5** When you feel you are free of these negative feelings, drink the water, and imagine yourself being filled with compassion, just as Kuan Yin is.

### NATURAL WATER

Kuan Yin holds the dew of compassion in a jar. You will need to symbolize this with fresh, cold water collected from a spring, or by putting a bowl outside to catch rainwater.

## RITUAL

# PURITY

*Set aside a day to purify yourself with the blessing of Kuan Yin. Spend the time alone, switch on the telephone answering machine, and turn off the television. Do not go out shopping, or anywhere else where you will have to deal with other people.*

### YOU WILL NEED

· Salt
· Fresh, organic fruit

**GIVE YOURSELF TIME**

Choose a day when you do not have to work, and when you have no other commitments. If this is impossible, try to organize as much free time for yourself as you can—a whole morning perhaps, or a whole evening.

1 At the beginning of the day, take a purifying bath containing a handful of salt. As you step into it, call on Kuan Yin, saying: "Kuan Yin, wash away my imperfections and leave me as pure as you are."

2 Spend the day doing simple things that you enjoy, especially thinking, reading, and being with nature. You might like to pick flowers, or go for a long country walk.

3 Drink only water and eat only fresh organic fruit.

4 At the end of the day, repeat the bath and mantra from Stage 1.

# LAKSHMI

*Hindu goddess of good fortune and beauty*

Lakshmi is the wife of Vishnu, the preserver. Vishnu has appeared in nine incarnations, including a fish, a turtle, a boar, and a lion; and Lakshmi, too, has appeared in many forms. They fly together through the sky on the back of the man-bird Garuda, who symbolizes the sun, or rest together upon Ananta, the many-headed serpent of eternity.

Lakshmi was born out of the foam of the sea at the Churning of the Ocean, when the gods became immortal by producing the elixir of life. She lives in great luxury surrounded by sumptuous fabrics, jewels, music, and animals. She is usually depicted wearing garlands of lotus blossoms, or sitting on a lotus blossom or peacock. She sometimes has four arms.

Lakshmi distributes good fortune randomly and not necessarily fairly. She confers, at her whim, beauty, happiness, wealth, and prosperity. She represents the model wife, and young brides dress as Lakshmi when their husbands bring them into the house. The brides wear jewels and a robe of gold—her symbol. In India, she is worshipped at the beginning of the business year, and each household lights a lamp for her during the Diwali festival—the Feast of Lamps.

## RITUAL

# HAPPINESS

*What is happiness? We all know we want it, but do we really know what would make us happy? For many of us it is love, but not for all. For some it is having enough money to be free from financial worries. Others are satisfied by having enough time to pursue their own interests. So, before asking Lakshmi for happiness, take some time to consider what it is that would make you happy.*

### YOU WILL NEED

- Gold clothing of some description
- A candle
- A brass or gold-colored lantern

#### GOLDEN ATTIRE

If you do not have any gold clothing, wear something with a gold trim, or drape yourself in a gold scarf or shawl. If possible, wear gold shoes and ribbons, and plenty of gold jewelry.

1 Wearing some kind of gold clothing, light the candle in the lantern, and hang the lantern in a window where it can be seen from outside.

2 Call on the goddess: "Lakshmi, you confer happiness at your will; will your happiness to fall on me."

3 Leave the lantern until the candle burns down, or until you go to bed.

4 Relight the same or a new candle in the lantern every evening for a month, to attract Lakshmi's attention to you.

# RITUAL

## BEGINNING A PROJECT

*Lakshmi can confer good fortune on anyone she pleases, but one of her special interests is business. This ritual is for the start of any project, but is especially apt if you are launching a business project.*

### YOU WILL NEED

· A deck of playing or angel cards

**ANGEL CARDS**

You can use a deck of playing cards or angel cards, in which each card bears a word such as "patience," "forgiveness," "courage," or "insight." You could make your own angel cards if you cannot find them to buy, but avoid tarot cards.

1 Shuffle the cards, and spread them out face down in front of you.

2 Draw one card and, as you do so, close your eyes and say: "Lakshmi, grant me your insight through the symbol of this card."

3 Now look at the card you have chosen; it might bear a number, a word, or an image. Whatever it is, look for it during your project and respond to it. Perhaps you have chosen the nine of clubs, so if you are offered business premises with the number nine in the address, for example, remember that nine is your lucky number. If you used angel cards, you will have a lucky word, which you should use in the same way. Do not reject Lakshmi's blessing—however unpromising or uninspiring the card may seem, do not change it, trust it.

84

# MAAT

*Egyptian goddess of truth, justice, and cosmic order*

Maat's symbol is the ostrich feather—the feather of truth—which she uses to judge the dead: each soul is brought to her, and she weighs its heart in the scales against her feather. Beside the scales squats a female monster who is known as the Devourer of the Dead. If the soul is lighter than the feather, it is allowed to pass on to the kingdom of Osiris—the underworld; if it is not, it is eaten by the monster. Maat is often depicted with an ostrich plume on her head because of her rule in this process.

Maat is also the goddess of cosmic order. She was present when the universe began, watching over the balance of everything, from the heavenly bodies to human relationships. She sees that the earth and the heavens operate harmoniously, and she regulates the seasons, the cycle of night and day, the rainfall, and the movement of the stars.

Maat is the overseer of social relationships, ethics, and good behavior. The rulers of Egypt considered themselves under Maat's protection, and liked to be described as "beloved of Maat." She figured prominently in the Egyptian system of justice, and judges always wore an effigy of her on their chests.

## RITUAL

# TRUTH

*This ritual will help you to live more honestly, and to experience more truthfulness around you. Many of us are less than truthful sometimes, and although the dishonesty is rarely meant to be harmful, the truth is regularly sidelined.*

### YOU WILL NEED

· A dark blue feather

#### CALL ON MAAT

When you call on Maat, she will help you to see how truth is compromised in many little ways every day, and to learn not to be a part of this dishonesty yourself.

-

Dark blue symbolizes truth, and the feather is a symbol of Maat, hence why we use a dark blue feather for this ritual.

1 Stand in front of a window, hold up the feather before you, and say: "Maat, let your feather of truth weigh up all that I do and say."

2 Now stand the feather upright in the window.

3 Spend the whole day making a conscious effort to be as honest as possible. If you are unhappy with someone or something, either say so or genuinely rid yourself of the feeling—don't pretend that everything is fine if it isn't. If anyone asks you for an opinion, be honest (without being unkind). Do not agree with people unless you really mean it; do not go along with things just for appearances.

## RITUAL

# JUSTICE

*Use this ritual if you are involved in a dispute in which you feel you are not receiving justice. It might be a conflict with friends or family, at work, or even a legal action.*

### YOU WILL NEED

· A black candle
· Pen and paper
· A white feather

**LISTEN TO MAAT**

Remember, if you call on Maat for justice, you must be prepared to accept the final outcome.

1 Light the candle, then take two pieces of paper.

2 On the first piece of paper outline the key points of the issue in question, from your point of view, and state briefly why you are so sure that you are in the right.

3 On the second piece of paper write down the same points from the other point of view, as if it were being written by the other party involved in the argument.

4 Place these two pieces of paper one on each side of the candle, and lie the feather on the table in front of the candle.

5 Now ask Maat for justice, saying: "Maat, you see and weigh up both sides of every argument. I ask you to see that justice is done, and I will accept your verdict."

# NUT

*Egyptian goddess of the sky*

---

Nut was the sister and consort of Geb, and the two held each other so closely that there was no room between them. Nut married Geb against the will of Ra, the sun god, who ordered the couple's father, Shu, the god of air, to separate the two deities. Shu held Nut up high above the earth to make room for living creatures below. Nut's belly is the sky, and the stars are the jewels on her robes. Geb forms the earth beneath her.

As an additional punishment, Ra decreed that Nut could not bear a child in any month of the year. However, Thoth, the scribe of the gods, played checkers with the moon to win a seventy-second portion of the moon's light, and with this he created five new days for Nut, who bore five children, one on each of the new days. She gave birth to three sons: Osiris, Seth, and Horus; and two daughters: Isis and Nephthys.

Nut is generally depicted as a naked, slim woman arched over and balanced on her toes and fingertips, which are touching the four cardinal compass points. She is the barrier between the earth and the cosmos. The solar boat carries the sun god Ra along her back each day, disappearing into her mouth at night. At dawn, it emerges again from her vulva to start anew its journey across the skies.

> *I will love the light
> for it shows me the way,
> yet I will endure the darkness
> because it shows me the stars.*
>
> —
>
> OG MANDINO

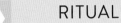

# RITUAL

## INFERTILITY

*Many couples have trouble conceiving a child. For some the problems are relatively short-lived; for others it can take years, often with many unpleasant tests and treatments. Others are unlucky and have to learn to find fulfillment elsewhere. This ritual calls on the goddess Nut, who also experienced problems bearing a child.*

### YOU WILL NEED

· Dark blue candle
· Star amulet

1 Stand in front of a lit dark blue candle, and hold up the star in front of the flame.

2 Invoke Nut's blessing by saying: "Nut, I ask you to bless me with a child. Help me to conceive or, if I must, to find fulfillment without a child."

3 If and when your child is born, bury the star—in a peaceful spot, at night—as an offering to Nut.

### STAR SYMBOL

Nut is the sky goddess and her belly is covered in stars, so an appropriate way to invoke her blessing is through the symbol of a star, which can also represent your wish for a child. Find a star amulet, such as a piece of jewelry in the shape of a star, or a silver pendant or object with a star engraved on it. Do not rush: let the right star symbol find you.

## GAINING TIME

*We have all sorts of reasons for wanting to make time, from frantic work deadlines to having longer vacations, or more time to spend gardening or with our grandchildren. The god Thoth created five new days so that Nut could bear her five children.*

### YOU WILL NEED

- An apple
- A fireproof bowl
- A length of blue silk ribbon

**RITUAL OF APPRECIATION**

This ritual will not actually create extra time, of course, but it will make the time you have seem longer, and it will help you to appreciate it so that you get more value from the time that you do have.

1 Cut the apple cleanly in half, then remove all the seeds—make sure that you find every single one—and put them in the bowl.

2 Take them outside and burn them (you may need some other flammable material, such as wood or paper, to help you do this).

3 Bind the two halves of the apple together again with the blue ribbon, and bury it outside.

4 Get rid of the remains of the seeds in a way that ensures that they can never sprout; you might throw them on a fire, or put them in a sealed container until your need for more time has passed.

*The butterfly counts
not months but moments,
and has time enough.*

—

**RABINDRANATH TAGORE**

# PAPA

*Maori goddess of the earth*

Papa is the wife of the sky god Rangi. Before there was light, these two deities were inextricably held together in a continuous embrace, so their children could not leave Papa's womb. In addition, their close embrace also prevented plants and fruits from growing on the earth.

Papa and Rangi's children argued about what to do. Some felt that they should kill their parents, but Tane, the forest god, advocated separating the pair, pushing Rangi away but keeping Papa close to them. All the children tried to do this, but failed. However, Tane eventually managed to force the two apart and into eternal separation. As they parted, the sky was filled with light. The Nghaitahu people of New Zealand's South Island used to say that the mists were the sighs of Papa and Rangi, and the morning dew was Rangi's tears of sorrow at their separation.

Papa is also worshipped in Hawaii, where they say she was married to the first chieftain, the human Wakea, but left him when he had an incestuous affair with one of their daughters. Papa was so angry that she deserted the earth and cursed humans with mortality. Her departure is also said to account for the class divisions in Hawaiian society, since one of the children she abandoned became the first slave.

## DIVORCE

*Even if it is you who have chosen divorce, it is never a happy decision.*
*Papa is a sympathetic goddess to invoke during these upsetting times,*
*since she understands the feelings associated with divorce.*

### YOU WILL NEED

· Compass

**RITUAL ON A HILLTOP**

Papa is an earth goddess, so it is easiest to get close to
her in the countryside. If you live in a city, try to set aside
a special day when you can travel out of town to a hill to
perform this ritual—ideally a place with a history of worship,
such as a stone circle or an ancient sacred site.

1 Sit on the summit of a hill and face west. Pick up a handful of soil, stones, or grass. Look at it, and think about all the negative emotions of the past few weeks and months from which you want to break free.

2 Then throw the contents of your hand as far down the hillside as you can, saying: "Papa, I call on you to take these feelings from me."

3 Now stand up, turn around, and face east. Look at the skyline and focus on the emotions that you no longer want to feel.

4 When you have finished, close your eyes and take three deep breaths before leaving the top of the hill.

*Our greatest glory is
not in never falling,
but in rising
every time we fall.*

—

CONFUCIUS

> *Peace is not absence of conflict,*
> *it is the ability to handle*
> *conflict by peaceful means.*
> —

RONALD REAGAN

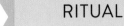

# RITUAL

## CONFLICT WITH CHILDREN

*This ritual calls on the earth goddess Papa, who came into conflict with her children. Stones are the children of the earth, and are used in this ritual to represent your child and yourself.*

### YOU WILL NEED

- Smooth stones
- A blue candle
- A box or pouch large enough to keep the stones in

**PAPA'S SYMBOLS**

Collect some smooth stones to which you feel drawn; you will need one for each of the people involved in the conflict. Select a stone to represent Papa, too.

-

A blue candle is used to represent friendship and cooperation.

1 Clean and buff the stones.

2 Light the blue candle, and arrange the stones around it in a clear pattern, such as a triangle, a square, or a circle. The important thing is that the pattern symbolizes order, so all the stones should be roughly equidistant from the candle.

3 Spend a few moments thinking about the relationship you would like to come out of this conflict.

4 Leave the stones around the candle until it has burnt down and gone out.

5 Put the stones together in a box or pouch, and keep them somewhere safe until the conflict is resolved. When it has passed, return the stones to the earth.

# PARVATI

*Hindu goddess of fertility*

---

Parvati is a benign aspect of Devi, the principal female goddess in the Hindu pantheon. She is a goddess of fertility and the consort of Shiva, god of destruction, and personifies the perfect, devoted, and steadfast wife. Parvati was once dark skinned, but Shiva goaded her so much that she went to great lengths to become golden skinned.

Parvati was originally introduced to Shiva as a dancing girl, but the ascetic god showed no interest in her since he was still mourning his first wife, Sati. However, Parvati was in fact a reincarnation of Sati. She pursued a life of self-denial alongside Shiva, until, finally, under the influence of the love god Kama, Shiva was filled with desire for Parvati and took her as his consort.

Parvati is the mother of Ganesha, the god of good fortune. She fashioned her son from the skin that she rubbed from her body while bathing, and created him expressly so that he could guard her. To that purpose, she set Ganesha outside her room. When Shiva arrived, Ganesha tried to prevent him from entering, so Shiva knocked his head off. Parvati was distraught, and insisted that Shiva restore her son to life. Shiva grabbed the nearest head he could find, that of an elephant, which is why Ganesha is an elephant-headed god.

## RITUAL

## SUPPORT IN PARTNERSHIP

*This ritual will help to strengthen your ability to support your partner. It will also bring Parvati's influence to bear on them, so that they too will be more supportive.*

### YOU WILL NEED

· Sweet-smelling oil or body moisturizer
· Music you like to dance to

**GET TOGETHER**
If possible, you and your partner should perform this ritual together.

1 Begin by taking a relaxing bath, and use this time to release any stresses and mental distractions.

2 When you have finished your bath, cover yourself with sweet-smelling oil or moisturizing cream.

3 Now play some music that you enjoy dancing to. It does not matter whether this is a classical waltz or a rock'n'roll song—just make sure it is happy music. Play it as loudly as you can (without upsetting your neighbors), and begin dancing. If you and your partner are performing the ritual together, dance in a way that entails touching and holding each other.

4 Dance around every room in the house, including the hallway, children's rooms, study, and stairway, but concentrate on the bedroom, kitchen, bathroom, and living room, and any other rooms where you and your partner spend the most time.

5 Continue dancing for as long as you have the energy to enjoy it.

# RITUAL

## PERSISTENCE

*Most of us find it hard to be persistent at times. Even if we are committed in some areas of our lives, there are others in which we have problems seeing things through. This ritual will help you acquire some of Parvati's astonishing powers of persistence.*

## YOU WILL NEED

· Pen and paper

### SELF-DENIAL

In order to learn from Parvati, give up something for a month, just as she gave up all comforts and luxuries for years to win Shiva's love. Choose something unrelated to your usual problem area—for instance, if you have trouble persisting with diets, give up television; if you have trouble working through relationship problems, give up alcohol or chocolate. Parvati will strengthen you through this ritual of self-denial.

1 Write down on a piece of paper what it is you are giving up.

2 On the first day of the month, ask Parvati to help you: "Parvati, you denied yourself for years; help me to persist for just one month in denying myself this one thing."

3 Hold the paper in your hand and repeat this invocation whenever you feel your resolve weakening.

GODDESS

# PROSERPINA

*Roman goddess of the underworld*

Proserpina, the beautiful Roman goddess of the underworld, is the daughter of Jupiter (king of the gods) and Ceres (goddess of the harvest). Her symbols are corn and the pomegranate. When she was young, her uncle Pluto, god of the underworld, fell in love with her. He kidnapped her with the collusion of his brother, Jupiter, and took her down to his kingdom.

When Ceres could not find her daughter she was heartbroken, and searched all over the earth for her. When eventually she discovered what had happened, Ceres was so angry that she withdrew her blessing from the earth, so the crops failed and there was a worldwide drought. Jupiter had to do something, so he sent his messenger Mercury to tell Pluto to release Proserpina. Pluto agreed, but before she left he gave her a pomegranate to eat. Proserpina swallowed one of the seeds, not realizing that if you eat the food of the dead you cannot leave the underworld.

Caught between this edict and Ceres' anger, Jupiter decreed that Proserpina must spend two-thirds of the year above the ground with her mother, and the remaining third with Pluto. Ceres lets nothing grow when her daughter is in the underworld, so it is winter; but when Proserpina rejoins her mother, Ceres permits the spring to blossom.

## RITUAL

# PATIENCE

*Most of us wish that we had more patience to help us through periods of waiting. It may be for the return of a loved one, for examination results to arrive, for a house sale to be completed, or even for the winter to be over. Proserpina was forced to spend every winter in the underworld against her will, but she endured it patiently.*

## YOU WILL NEED

- A black candle
- A blindfold (optional)

**DARKNESS**

This ritual invokes the goddess Proserpina by symbolizing her imprisonment under the ground; it should be performed after dark, in a room in which you can block out as much light as possible.

1 Light the candle, then close the drapes and turn out any other lights.

2 Sit down in front of the candle, noticing how reliant on it you are. Then blow it out, leaving yourself in total darkness; if necessary, put on a blindfold made from a black silk or chiffon scarf.

3 Sit in darkness for about fifteen minutes (or as near as you can estimate), meditating on what Proserpina had to endure for four months every year. Silently ask her to give you some of her patience.

## RITUAL

# SUNNY WEATHER

*Proserpina spends one-third of the year below ground, during which time it is winter, but when she finally resurfaces, she brings the spring sunshine with her. This ritual calls on her to do the same for us, and to bring sunny weather.*

### YOU WILL NEED

- A piece of fruit to represent the sun
- An earthenware bowl
- Sand

**SUN FRUIT**

For this ritual you will need a piece of fruit that symbolizes the sun. A pomegranate is ideal, since it is associated with Proserpina, but if you cannot find one of these, use an orange or a lemon.

1 Begin by dedicating the fruit to Proserpina, by simply saying: "Proserpina, I dedicate this pomegranate (or orange or lemon) to you."

2 Place the fruit in the bottom of the bowl and cover it with sand until none of it is showing. Leave it for a couple of hours while you do other things.

3 Return to the bowl and uncover the fruit. As you lift it from beneath the sand, invoke the goddess, saying: "As you rise each spring from the ground, as this pomegranate (or orange or lemon) rises from the sand, so let the sun rise in the sky and shine warm upon us."

4 Now eat the fruit to feel the goddess's energy inside you.

# SEDNA

### *Inuit goddess of the sea*

---

Sedna is an Inuit sea goddess who rules over the deep oceans where men are sent to atone for their sins; she also rules the dead who live there. Although the Inuits feared her greatly, they nevertheless appealed to her, through their shamans, to provide seals for them to hunt. Sedna was originally a beautiful young woman, who turned down every man who came to court her. Her father, however, needed a strong young man in the family and insisted that she marry the next one who proposed to her. A man soon appeared, his face and head hidden by furs, and promised Sedna a warm home and plenty of money. She reluctantly agreed to marry him, but when they reached his house, it was cold and bleak. The man then removed his hood, revealing a hideous face. At that very moment he turned into a storm petrel, a sea bird, and flew off.

Sedna's father rescued his daughter, but the petrel pursued them. Her father was so afraid that the bird would raise a storm to kill them both that, to save himself, he threw Sedna overboard. She clung to the side of the boat but he cut off her fingers—these became seals, walruses, and whales. With no way of holding on, she sank. Sedna now lies under the sea, guarding her sea creatures and raising storms to drown men.

# FORGIVENESS

*Guilt is one of the most destructive emotions, whether it is justified or not. It benefits no one, yet it can be hard to shake off. Sometimes we can ask forgiveness from the person we believe we have hurt, but at other times this is not possible; sometimes it is not a person we want forgiveness from, but a higher spirit. The goddess Sedna, who rules over the land of the dead, bestows forgiveness on those who feel remorse. This ritual will help ease your guilt when you feel troubled.*

## YOU WILL NEED

• A simple meal of fish and vegetables
• Candles

### SIMPLE MEAL

Cook yourself a simple meal of fish, perhaps steamed or baked; this embodies Sedna's spirit. You could accompany it with a few steamed vegetables.

1 Sit down to eat the meal by candlelight, so that you can focus your thinking.

2 As you eat, think of a person against whom you hold a grudge, and consciously and genuinely forgive them. If you can, think of someone whose behavior is in some way comparable to the behavior about which you yourself feel guilty.

3 In exchange for giving someone else forgiveness, you can now ask Sedna for hers: "Sedna, by eating this fish, let me bring your spirit inside me to cleanse me of guilt."

# RITUAL

## SEARCHING

*This ritual is not about finding lost objects, but about the search for yourself: who are you, and what do you really want? It is a search that drives many of us, and it often takes years to discover the answer. Sedna is the patron goddess of the Inuit hunters as they search for food, and she can help you to find the answers if you ask her.*

### YOU WILL NEED

· Your choice of artistic tools
· Recorded whale song

**OCEAN SOUNDS**

This ritual will take a few evenings to complete, perhaps four or five over the course of a week or so, or longer if you wish. At each session you should listen to whale song—downloaded or on CD—in honor of Sedna.

1 Over the course of several evenings, and while listening to whale song, embroider, paint, sculpt, or draw a whale, designing it however you choose—it might be a group of whales, a seascape with a whale in the distance, or a close-up of one.

2 At the start of each session, ask yourself: "What am I seeking, and why?"

3 As you create the whale artwork, and listen to the whale song, meditate on your search.

4 By the time you have finished your work of art, you should be much closer to finding your answer.

# TARA

*Tibetan goddess of wisdom and compassion*

Tara is the great mother goddess of Tibetan Buddhism, and the wife of Avalokitesvara—the original bodhisattva who achieved enlightenment but rejected a life in Nirvana in favor of staying on earth to help humans. According to legend, the Tibetan people—and even the Buddha himself—are descended from Tara and Avalokitesvara.

Tara is deeply compassionate, and particularly concerned for people who are in danger at sea; she is sometimes described as the "mistress of boats." However, her greatest gift is wisdom. She helps those in contemplation and meditation on their journey to enlightenment, and leads her followers over the river of experience to the land of spiritual freedom. Tara often appears sitting on a lion and holding up the sun, or as a young woman holding a lotus flower.

Tara can appear in many aspects, each of which has a different color. Her gentlest colors are white and green, but she can be dangerous in her red, yellow, or blue aspect. For example, Yellow Tara is Bhrkuti, mother of the Buddha, a cruel aspect with three eyes. On the other hand, Green Tara is said to have been born from a teardrop of Avalokitesvara, and is believed to make worldly anxieties disappear.

# RITUAL

## INSIGHT INTO A LOVER'S HEART

*Many of us experience times of uncertainty regarding how strongly a lover feels about us. This simple ritual calls on Tara to enlighten us about a lover's true feelings.*

### YOU WILL NEED

· Pen and paper

**TRUST YOURSELF**
This ritual requires only a pen and a sheet of paper, and the ability to trust your subconscious mind. Do the ritual at a time when you are relaxed.

1 Sit down with the pen and paper in your hand, and close your eyes.

2 Focus on your lover's name, and physical and emotional characteristics. Open your eyes and write TARA in the center of the sheet of paper.

3 Focusing your mind on your lover, begin to doodle their name around the page, along with anything else that comes into your mind. You can doodle words, pictures, or abstract designs. Allow your mind to wander as you slowly fill up the whole page with doodles.

4 When you have filled the page, put down the pen and focus again on your lover. Look over your doodles until something jumps out at you. This is a clue, and you will need to peruse it until your mind makes a link that gives you insight into your lover's true feelings.

## RITUAL

## SAFETY IN TRAVEL

*This ritual calls on Tara to keep you safe on a journey, but you can adapt it to protect someone else if you wish.*

### YOU WILL NEED

· A white candle
· A model vehicle

**1** Clear a reasonably large table, leaving nothing on it except the white candle.

**2** Light the candle, pick up the model vehicle in your left hand, and say: "Tara, this is the journey I shall take."

**3** Now push (or fly) the vehicle across the table from left to right, and, as you do so, visualize it following the journey you will be taking. Imagine that it is turning off the highway, or crossing a bridge, or flying over the sea.

**4** Do not worry about incorporating every tiny detail of a long journey, but include what you can to make it feel like a complete representation of your trip. If you reach the far side of the table before you arrive at your destination, just carry on around the table.

**5** When you reach the end, say: "Tara, protect and keep me safe to the end of my journey."

> **SAFE TRANSPORT**
> You will need a model or representation of the kind of transport you will be using for the journey—for example, a toy car, boat, train, or airplane.
>
> —
>
> The white candle represents safety.

# VENUS

*Roman goddess of love and the spring*

The best-known goddess of love, Venus is the Roman counterpart of the Greek goddess Aphrodite. She is the daughter of Jupiter, and was born out of the foam of the sea. Her chariot is a scallop shell drawn by dolphins.

Venus was made to bestow love, and had several consorts. These included Vulcan, god of fire, and the war god Mars, who fathered her son Cupid, the love god. However, her most passionate attachment was to Adonis, the god of vegetation. Venus rescued the motherless Adonis as a baby because he was so beautiful. She was determined to keep him safe, so she hid him in a casket, which she gave to the goddess of the underworld, Proserpina, to look after. However, when Proserpina opened the casket, she saw how beautiful Adonis was and decided to keep him for herself.

Venus appealed to the gods for help. Her father, Jupiter, eventually decided that Adonis should spend half of each year in the underworld with Proserpina, and the other half in the world above with Venus. As Adonis grew up, he and Venus were passionate lovers, but each winter she lost him. However, when spring returned each year they were reunited. For this reason, Venus is also the goddess of the spring, and her festival is celebrated on April 1st.

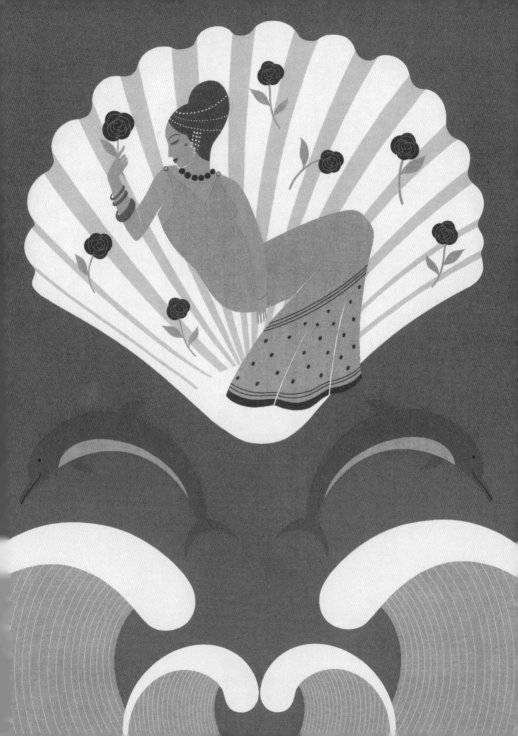

> *I believe in the immeasurable power of love; that true love can endure any circumstance and reach across any distance.*

STEVE MARABOLI

# RITUAL

## SEPARATION IN LOVE

*This ritual is for those times when you are separated from your partner, perhaps by work, and symbolizes the reunion you want with your loved one. It gives you strength and patience to endure the separation, just as Venus endured separation from her lover Adonis, and makes the time go faster until you are together again.*

## YOU WILL NEED

· A red candle
· Two flat heart shapes modeled by hand

### MODELING HEARTS

You will need to use some kind of modeling material, such as clay, wax, or dough, to mold two flat heart shapes; you could roll out the clay or dough and then use a heart-shaped cutter to cut the two shapes.

1 Light the red candle. As the wax begins to melt, drip it onto one of the heart shapes.

2 While the wax is still warm, press the other heart on top of it like a sandwich, so that the wax glues the two hearts together. As you do this, say: "Venus, goddess of love, bring my love back to me safe and soon."

3 Keep repeating this invocation as you drip the wax and bind the hearts together.

4 Keep your heart token somewhere safe until you are reunited with your loved one.

> *When all the world appears to be in a tumult, and nature itself is feeling the assault of climate change, the seasons retain their essential rhythm. Yes, fall gives us a premonition of winter, but then, winter, will be forced to relent, once again, to the new beginnings of soft greens, longer light, and the sweet air of spring.*

MADELEINE M. KUNIN

## RITUAL

# WELCOMING THE SPRING

*It is important to mark the seasons, as it keeps us in tune with the earth's cycles, and with our own. The start of spring sets off a response in us, just as it does with other animals and plants. Spring is a time of love, so it is appropriate that Venus, the goddess of spring, is also a love goddess.*

## YOU WILL NEED

· A packet of seeds
· A scallop shell

**THE SCENT OF SPRING**

If you are tuned to the seasons, you can tell when spring arrives—there will be one day when you step outside, breathe in, and you can literally smell the change in the air. Look out for this day, breathing the air deeply each morning so that you know when it arrives.

1 To welcome the spring, take a packet of seeds that, in your mind, represent the time of year or Venus herself. Plants associated with love are a good choice, such as love-in-a-mist (*Nigella damascena*).

2 Empty the seeds into the scallop shell (a symbol of Venus), and sprinkle them on the ground in the place you want them to grow.

## GODDESS

# XOCHIQUETZAL

*Aztec goddess of flowers, love, and craftmanship*

The goddess of flowers and love, singing and dancing, Xochiquetzal's name means "flower petal." Everywhere she goes she is followed by butterflies and birds. She lives on a mountain and presides over the twentieth day of the Aztec calendar. Once every eight years the Aztecs would hold a great feast in Xochiquetzal's honor, when everyone wore animal and flower masks.

Xochiquetzal is young, beautiful, charming, and flirtatious. She is well aware of her charms, and uses them knowingly. A fertility goddess with a strong sexuality, Xochiquetzal took her brother Xochipilli as her lover. This adulterous affair explains why she is the patron goddess of harlots. She is also the patroness of pregnant women and childbirth, as well as of the moon and craftspeople. The Aztecs often invoked her to make a marriage fruitful: the bride plaited her hair and then coiled it around her head, leaving two plumes of "feathers" like the tail of the quetzal, a bird that is sacred to the goddess.

Xochiquetzal is the mother of the snake-bird god Quetzalcoatl, who descended into the underworld. (The Aztecs believed that Quetzalcoatl would return one day. It was in the belief that Hernando Cortez was the returning god that the Aztecs at first welcomed the Spanish, with disastrous consequences.) This probably explains Xochiquetzal's association with the underworld; it is also why the Aztecs made offerings of marigold garlands to her during festivals of the dead.

## RITUAL

## SINGING AND DANCING

*This ritual will increase your talent at singing and dancing, and will also boost your enjoyment of it. Xochiquetzal is young, beautiful, and sensual, so invoking her with this ritual will make you more sexually attractive as a singer and a dancer.*

### YOU WILL NEED

· Craft materials and equipment of your choice
· Elastic
· Decorations of your choice

**ANIMAL MASK**
The Aztecs celebrated Xochiquetzal at a great feast, where they wore animal and flower masks. For this ritual you will make yourself a similar mask out of cardboard, stiffened fabric, or leather; an eye mask is all you need, but you can make a full face mask if you wish.

1 Design and cut a mask shape of your choosing.

2 Thread elastic through holes in the upper corners so that the mask will stay in place around your head.

3 Decorate the mask to resemble a bird, butterfly, or other animal. If possible, incorporate something real from the animal in question into the mask—for instance, put some feathers on a bird mask, a snipping of cat's fur on a cat mask, and so on.

4 Now wear the mask as you sing and dance around your house or yard, and as you do so, feel Xochiquetzal's lightness and spirit within you.

## RITUAL

# SUCCESS IN CRAFTSMANSHIP

*Xochiquetzal is the patron goddess of craftspeople. This ritual asks for her blessing on you as a metalworker, joiner, silversmith, or whatever craft you practice. Invoke her to make the work you produce successful, but in particular for financial success at your craft.*

### YOU WILL NEED

‣ Marigolds or paper flowers and string

#### FLOWERS
One of the traditional offerings for Xochiquetzal is a garland of marigold flowers. Ideally, you should grow these yourself. If you cannot grow them, you may be able to buy or borrow them. Failing this, make paper flowers out of orange tissue paper.

1 If using real flowers, string them into a garland as if making a daisy chain, or thread paper flowers onto a string.

2 Stand outside facing into the sun, hold the garland up above your head and dedicate it to Xochiquetzal by saying: "Xochiquetzal, I offer you this garland as a token of respect and love. Please bless me in return with success in my chosen craft."

3 Then hang the garland above the place where you work at your craft.

# INDEX

Goddesses are in **bold**. Rituals have *italic* page numbers.

**A**

Actaeon 30
Adonis 116
Ananta 80
Anat 12
animals 34, 37, *37*, 80
Apollo 30
appreciation ritual *92*
artistic success ritual *19*
Asgard (Fensalir) 44
**Astarte** 12–15
**Athena** 16–19
Athirat 12
Avalokitesvara 112

**B**

Baal 12
Balder 44, 56
**Bastet** 20–5
bathing ritual *15, 32, 79*
beauty 38, 80
beginning a project ritual *83*
bereavement ritual *60*
birds 16, 62, 84
blindfolds 106
bodhisattva, Buddhist 76, 112
bowls 51, 60, 78, 92, 107
boxes 14, 43, 69, 99

**C**

candles 15, 41, 60, 82
    black 51, 87, 106
    colored 43, 59, 91, 99, 119
    white 32, 73, 115
cards, playing/angel *83*
cats 20, 23, 30, 33
Ceres 104
**Chalchiuhtlicue** 26–9
chastity ritual *32*

childbirth 30, *33*, 62, 122
children *54, 99*
clothing 18, 32, 41, 69, 82
coins 43
colors 18, 112
compass 88, 96
compassion 76, *78*, 112
conflict *65, 98*
cosmic order 84
cows 52, 54, 70
craftmanship 122, 124, *125*
creative pursuits 16, 19, 23
crystal, rock 54

**D**

dagger 38
dance 52, 102
darkness 106
Devi 100
**Diana** 30–3
divorce ritual *96*

**E**

earth 47, 48, 51, 94
El 12
Ephesus 30
**Epona** 34–7
**Ezili** 38–43

**F**

faithfulness ritual *69*
feathers 65, 84, 86, 87, 122
fertility 20, 26, 34, 44, 52, 66, 70, 100, 122
fish 110
flowers and plants 28, 32, 37, 44, 51, 76, 112, 122, 125
focus, objects of 8
forgiveness ritual *110*
fortune, good *46*, 80
**Frigga** 44–7
fruit and vegetables 16, 28, 50, 79, 92, 107, 110

**G**

**Gaia** 48–51
Ganesha 100
garlands 125
Garuda 80
Geb 88
gentleness ritual *23*
Gilgamesh 66
Gna 44

**H**

hair, lock of 69
happiness ritual *82*
harvest time 50
**Hathor** 12, 20, 52–5
Hawaii 94
healing 34, *36*
hearts 38, 119
**Hel** 56–61
**Hera** 62–5
hilltop ritual *96*
horn of plenty 34
horses 34
horseshoes 37
Horus 52
hunting 30

**I**

infertility ritual *91*
insight into a lover's heart ritual *114*
intimate items 69
**Ishtar** 66–9
**Isis** 70–5

**J**

Jason 62
jewelry 18, *33*, 41, 73
Jupiter 104, 116
justice 84, *87*

**K**
Kama 100
keys 44, 46
Kronos 48
**Kuan Yin** 76–9

**L**
**Lakshmi** 80–3
lanterns 82
lions 20, 23, 66, 112
Loki 56
love 38, 44, 52, 116, 122
loyalty ritual 73

**M**
**Maat** 84–7
marriage 28, 44, 48, 51, 62, 76, 80
masks 124
mementoes 55, 60
Mercury 104
mercy 76
Midgard worm 56
milk 54, 74
model vehicle 115
moisturizer, body 41, 102
mood, creating the 9
moon, the 24, 30, 122
Mot 12
motherhood 44, 75
mummification 70
music 33, 52, 102, 111

**N**
nature 48, 50, 75
night-time noise 24
**Nut** 88–93

**O**
oaths 48, 51
ocean sounds 111
offerings 28
oils, scented 15, 41, 102
Osiris 70
Ouranos 48

**P**
**Papa** 94–9
**Parvati** 100–3
patience ritual 106
pen and paper 36, 60, 87, 103, 114

persistence ritual 103
pharaohs 52
Pluto 104
pomegranate 62, 64, 104, 107
Poseidon 16
pouches 14, 29, 33, 43, 99
pregnancy 74, 122
**Proserpina** 104–7, 116
prosperity ritual 43
protection 20, 24, 29, 33, 47, 64
purity ritual 79

**Q**
Quetzalcoatl 122

**R**
Ra 52, 70, 88
Rangi 94
rattles 24, 54
relaxation ritual 15
ribbon/thread/string 36, 54, 69, 92

**S**
safe space 65
safety through the night ritual 14
salt 79
sand 107
sandalwood incense 54
Sati 100
sea, the 108, 112
searching ritual 111
**Sedna** 108–11
seeds 47, 121
Sekhmut 20
self-denial 103
separation in love ritual 119
Seth 70
sexual love/passion 41, 66, 68
shells, scallop 121
Shiva 100
shrines 20, 34, 75
Shu 88
sickness 59, 59
Sin (moon god) 66
singing and dancing ritual 124
sky, the 44, 88
sphinx 12
spring, the 116, 121, 121
star symbol 91

stones 28, 29, 73, 99
subconscious mind 114
sun, the 12, 74, 107, 107, 112
support in partnership ritual 102

**T**
talisman 14, 29
Tammuz 66
**Tara** 112–15
Thoth 88
time 79, 92
Tin Hau 76
Titans 48
Tlaloc 26
travel 55, 115
truth 84
truth ritual 86

**U**
underworld 56, 84, 104, 122

**V**
veils 59, 62
**Venus** 116–21
Virgin Mary 38
virginity 30, 66
Vishnu 80
visualization 68
Vodou gods 38

**W**
Wakea 94
war 16, 66
water sources 26, 28, 34, 68, 78
willow branches 76, 78
wisdom 18, 112
witchcraft/magic 20, 30, 70
womanhood 26, 70, 80

**X**
Xochipilli 122
**Xochiquetzal** 122–5

**Z**
Zeus 16, 48, 62